THE SIX-DAY WAR

The Conflict that Re-Shaped the Middle East

Written by Héloïse Malisse
In collaboration with Laure Delacroix
Translated by Carly Probert

History 50MINUTES.com

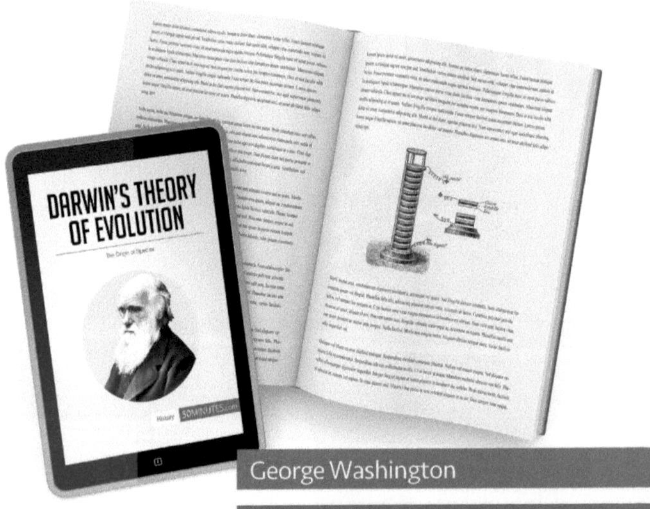
50MINUTES.com

BECOME AN EXPERT
IN HISTORY

DARWIN'S THEORY
OF EVOLUTION
The Origin of Species
History 50MINUTES.com

George Washington

The Battle of Austerlitz

Neil Armstrong

The Six-Day War

The Fall of Constantinople

www.50minutes.com

THE SIX-DAY WAR

KEY INFORMATION

- **When:** 5-10 June 1967
- **Where:** In the Sinai Peninsula, the West Bank and the Golan Heights (Northern Israel)
- **Context:** The Arab-Israeli conflict and the Israeli-Palestinian conflict
- **Belligerents:** Israel against Egypt, Jordan and Syria
- **Commanders and leaders:**
  - Levi Eshkol, Israeli Prime Minister (1895-1969)
  - Moshe Dayan, Israeli Defense Minister (1915-1981)
  - Gamal Abdel Nasser, President of the Republic of Egypt (1918-1970)
- **Outcome:** Israeli victory
- **Victims:**
  - Israeli camp: approximately 829 dead
  - Egyptian camp: between 5 000 and 10 000 dead
  - Jordanian camp: 700 dead and 550 taken prisoner
  - Syrian camp: 450 dead and 570 taken prisoner

INTRODUCTION

A major crisis in the Arab-Israeli conflict and the Israeli-Palestinian conflict, the Six-Day War began on 5 June 1967. The Israelis wanted to take preventive action against Egypt, the main military threat to the Jewish state, following the blockade of the Straits of Tiran (west of the Arabian Peninsula). The Egyptian air force was wiped out in just three hours and the Israeli army was then able to walk to the Sinai. The entire Arab world was outraged, condemned this attack and supported Egypt: Jordan and Syria joined the fight by attacking the Jewish state, and other countries, such as Lebanon and Iraq, sent material or human assistance. It should be noted that, at the time of the events, the Palestinian territories were controlled in part by Syria, Jordan and Egypt.

Six days later, after several cease-fires favoring Israel, the geopolitics of the Middle East had changed, and Israel was now in a dominant position compared to that of its Arab neighbors and saw its territory quadruple in size.

POLITICAL AND SOCIAL CONTEXT

A FORTY-YEAR-OLD CONFLICT

When the Six-Day War took place, tensions between the Jews and the Arabs had already existed for many years.

From the late 19th century, the Zionist movement began gradually restoring the Jewish state in Palestine, in response to various anti-Semitic waves of violence raging in Europe. Small Jewish farming communities were formed here and there until 1901, the year in which the Zionist movement created the Jewish National Fund for the purchase of land in Palestine, which then belonged to the Ottoman Empire. Seeing no advantage in this, the Ottoman Empire decided to severely restrict the development of Jewish villages in its territory. It was not until after the First World War (1914-1918) that the situation turned around for the Zionists. With the defeat of the Ottoman Empire that had fought along-side Germany, all Arab territories – i.e. Saudi, Iraq, Lebanon, Palestine and Syria – fell under British and French mandates. The British, with the Balfour Declaration of 2 November 1917, were in favor of the establishment of a national home for the Jewish people in Palestine and committed themselves to contributing to the realization of this project. Jewish immigration to Palestine became increasingly significant and continued to accelerate with the rise to power of Adolf Hitler (1889-1945) and the birth of Nazism in the early 1930s.

From 1920-1967, there were three major crises of the Arab-Israeli conflict:

- the Arab revolt in Palestine (1936-1938)
- the War of Independence (1948)
- the crisis of the Suez Canal (1956).

THE ARAB REVOLT (1936-1938)

The Arab revolt that took place in 1936 aimed to create an independent state in mandatory Palestine (i.e. under British mandate).

Arab revolt against British occupation.

After murders on both sides, a worrying sign of violence between Arabs and Jews, Britain decreed a state of emergency and imposed a curfew. Tensions continued to intensify and a general strike was organized throughout the country. The revolt gradually spread outside the borders and Syrian fighters came to stand alongside the Palestinians. Given this situation and the urgency to find a solution, the British proposed the formation of two states: the first, the Jewish state, would include Galilee (northern Israel) and the entire coastline; the second, the Palestinian state, would consist of the remaining territories annexed by Transjordan (now the West Bank). With the proposal rejected by the Arabs and by some Zionists, British policy hardened by repressing and imprisoning the principal leaders of the revolt. This first crisis still had a positive result as it allowed for the drafting of a series of laws in 1939, united under the name of the "White Paper", to regulate Jewish immigration to Palestine and the purchase of Arab land by Jews.

THE 1948 WAR OF INDEPENDENCE

The second crisis is what the Israelis called the War of Independence, or the Palestine War. It took place in 1948, when the British mandate came to an end following the adoption by the UN of the partition plan of Palestine a year earlier. The plan was rejected by the Palestinians, while the Jews wanted to secure land assigned to them, according to what was decided, by expelling the Arabs from it. This prompted a series of struggles, but the Jews, who were better prepared from a military point of view since their participation in the Second World War (1939-1945) alongside the British, prevailed. This was followed by an exodus of the Palestinian people, while Israel was proclaimed on 14 May 1948. The next day, in order to support the Palestinians, the Egyptian, Syrian, Iraqi, Jordanian and Lebanese armies declared war on Israel. After intense fighting and territorial conquests which, initially, benefitted the Arabs, the situation reversed and finally armistices were signed between the countries in February 1949. They drew new borders for Israel, which, emerging victorious, now held 78% of Palestine, including:

- Galilee
- the coastal territories of Palestine, with the exception of the Gaza Strip
- West Jerusalem
- the Negev desert.

THE CRISIS OF THE SUEZ CANAL (1956)

A few years later, in the context of the Cold War (1945-1990), a new crisis arose in the relationship between the Jews and the Arabs: the Suez Canal that pitted Egypt to Israel, Great Britain and France. That year, Egyptian President Gamal Abdel Nasser led a major campaign to improve the economic situation of his country. With the desire to build a dam on the Nile in order to regulate the river, he requested financial assistance from the United States, which was refused due to the fact that he maintained friendly relations with the Soviets. Therefore, the Egyptian President decided to nationalize the Suez Canal in order to reap the benefits it would provide for the construction of the dam.

Britain, France and Israel reacted immediately to this nationalization by launching a military attack on 29 October 1956. Israel thus conquered the Gaza Strip, then under Egyptian administration, and the Sinai. The UN condemned this attack in turn on 1 November and demanded a cease-fire. Although Israel submitted to this decision, the other two countries did not, and would ultimately be summed by the United States and the Soviet Union to abandon their military maneuvers. The truce was then accepted by Britain and France on 6 November 1956. Israel was therefore obliged to give up the conquered territories, but still obtained from the UN the presence of peacekeepers (members of the military forces of the UN) along the Israeli-Egyptian border.

THE SIXTIES AND RUMORS OF WAR

During the sixties, nuclear weapon development research by the Jewish state once again tarnished the Arab-Israeli relations. On 12 March 1966, the Cairo newspaper *Al Jumhuria* published the idea that "[a] preventive war is the only way to stop Israel from becoming a nuclear power" (Razoux

2004, p. 13). The fear of a nuclear conflict spread, especially among the Egyptians, who believed that they would be the first affected. Nasser then decided to take action on the planning of military operations in order to prevent such a disaster from happening. However, the wish of the Egyptian president was not to destroy the Jewish state: his only aim was to eliminate the nuclear threat by attempting to wipe out Israel's nuclear plants.

Meanwhile, the Israeli government was also planning military operations against its Arab neighbors, particularly against Egypt. Indeed, the Israelis feared being caught off guard by a surprise attack, as had almost been the case with the *Rotem* crisis (meaning "broom" in Hebrew) which occurred in February 1960 when Egypt installed around 15 000 soldiers and almost 500 tanks along the Israel-Egypt border, all without being noticed by the Israelis. It was not until four days later that the Israelis set up an operation to establish an armored division and position the entire Israeli air force in front of the Egyptian army. Although both parties were content to observe, this episode stuck in Israeli memories.

A NEW WAR WAS LOOMING

Following the frequent clashes between the Syrians and Jordanians with Israel in late 1966 and early 1967, Syrian President Ahmad Nureddin al-Atassi (1929-1992) and King Hussein of Jordan (1935-1999) continued to ask for Egyptian aid, while reproaching Gamal Abdel Nasser for his inaction. Finally, on 12 May 1967, as a result of Russian rumors of a large concentration of Israeli troops along the Syrian border, the Egyptian president decreed a general mobilization of his troops by invoking the socialist solidarity that bound Syria and Egypt. He thus ordered the shipment to Syria of several squadrons of Egyptian bombers. Two days later, on 14 May, he announced the strengthening of the Egyptian military presence in the Sinai Peninsula along the Israeli border. He also proclaimed the closure of the Tiran Strait on 22 May, preventing Israel from accessing the Red Sea. At the same time, he managed to secure the withdrawal of UN peacekeepers stationed along the Israeli-Egyptian border. For the Israeli people, these last two actions were considered a *casus belli* and the anguish of an imminent major conflict was looming.

COMMANDERS AND LEADERS

GAMAL ABDEL NASSER, PRESIDENT OF EGYPT

Portrait of Gamal Abdel Nasser.

Nasser was a statesman and President of the Republic of Egypt from 1956 to 1970. Prior to his political career, he served in the army and commanded a battalion in the Egyptian expeditionary forces during the 1948 war against Israel. In

1951, he was promoted to colonel. It was also at this time that he became one of the leaders of the Association of Free Officers that overthrew King Farouk I of Egypt in a military coup in July 1952. After dismissing his opponents of power, Gamal Abdel Nasser was elected president in January 1956, for which he was the only candidate. He was reelected in the same way until his death in 1970. His policy was described as Arab socialism. He was also the *rais* (meaning "chief" in Arabic) of the movement called Pan-Arabism.

GOOD TO KNOW

It was the *Baath* party (Arabic, meaning "resurrection") which prompted the Pan-Arab movement. Created in Syria in 1947, it was renamed the "Party of the Arab Socialist Resurrection" a few years later. This is an ideology that defends the need to unite the Arab world as one nation through the unity of language and civilization, not by religion, as was the case under the Ottoman Empire: Pan-Arabism is secular by definition.

During the few months before the Six-Day War, Syria sought the help of Egypt for the resolution of conflicts taking place along the Israeli-Syrian border, calling for Arab solidarity. Gamal Abdel Nasser protested merely verbally at first, but very soon he became a laughing stock among the other Arab leaders and was accused of inaction. For fear of losing credibility as the *rais* of Pan-Arabism, he decided to openly threaten Israel with his troops in Sinai.

Following the attack of the Egyptian air bases by an Israeli aircraft on 5 June, indignation affected all the Arab countries and Nasser recovered his popularity once again by becoming the figurehead of Arab thinking. From then on, he promised the destruction of Israel. He was supported by many at the beginning of the war and he was sent troops or material support.

At the end of the war, after a stinging defeat, the Egyptian president publicly took responsibility for the failure of the Arab armies and announced his resignation, which was denied by the Egyptian people. He then participated in the Arab summit in Khartoum (29 August-1 September 1968) and then engaged in a war of attrition against Israel in February 1969. Thus, he maintained an atmosphere of military tension all along the Suez Canal. This war of attrition was not completed until August 1970, when the Israelis agreed to a cease-fire. Nasser died shortly after from a heart attack.

LEVI ESHKOL, ISRAELI PRIME MINISTER

Portrait of Levi Eshkol.

An Israeli statesman born in Ukraine, Levi Eshkol immi-grated to Palestine in 1914, where he worked as a farmer in a *kibbutz* (collective agricultural Jewish village). In the twenties, he was one of the founders of the *Histadrut* company that set up the water distribution network in Israel. A member of *Mapai*, the Workers' Party of Israel (left wing), he was appointed deputy to the Defense Minister during the 1948 war. In 1951, he was elected to Israel's Assembly, the *Knesset*, on which he sat until his death. From 1952-1963, he served as Finance Minister before becoming Prime Minster and then Defense Minister.

During the tense period before the Six-Day War, Levi Eshkol refused to choose the warrior way of solving the situation. Only under Israeli public pressure did he decide to give up his post as Minister of Defense to Moshe Dayan, while allowing the leader of the Liberal Party *Herouth* (right wing) to enter the national unity government to plan in the best possible way the preparations for what would become the Six-Day War.

Criticized for his inaction during the crisis, Levi Eshkol remained at the head of the Israeli government until his death in 1969.

MOSHE DAYAN, ISRAELI DEFENSE MINISTER

Portrait of Moshe Dayan.

An Israeli military man and politician, General Moshe Dayan was born in 1915 in a *kibbutz* in Palestine. While still very young, he joined the *Haganah* (which means "defense" in Hebrew), a clandestine organization that militarily protected Jewish migrants from any Arab attacks. Imprisoned by the British in 1939 for illegal possession of firearms, he was released two years later to fight for the British army in the conquest of Lebanon. It was during this war that he lost his left eye following a serious injury, which he then hid with a black eye patch that made his face unforgettable on the international stage.

He also participated in the 1948 war, where he commanded a battalion, and the various conflicts in which Israel was involved until 1957, when he entered politics in the ranks of the left-wing *Mapai* party. Minister of Agriculture from 1959 to 1964, he resigned following opinion incompatibility with Prime Minister Levi Eshkol. On the eve of the Six-Day War, he was appointed Defense Minister, under the pressure of public opinion, which was reassured by the idea of having a war hero at the head of military affairs. During the conflict, he led the military operations in consultation with Yitzhak Rabin (Israeli officer and politician, 1922-1995), who was then the Chief of Staff of the IDF, the Israeli army. He remained Defense Minister until 1974, when he was forced to leave his post after the surprise attack of the Egyptian army during the Yom Kippur War of 1973, which strongly tainted his public image. He eventually retired from politics in 1979 and died two years later.

ANALYSIS OF THE WAR

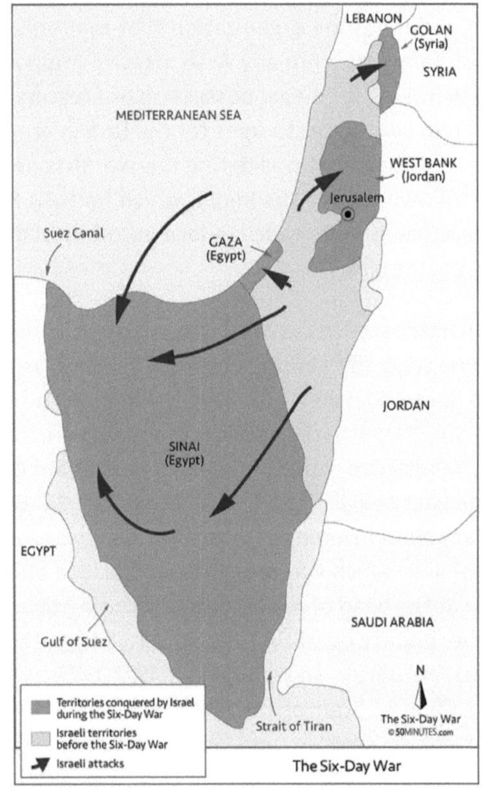

COMPOSITION AND STRATEGIES OF THE FORCES

The two opposing armies during the Six-Day War were radically different: while the Arabs emphasized quantity over quality, the Israelis preferred to rely on men who had the necessary military skills. Thus, no less than 215 000 Arab soldiers enlisted for the Six-Day War, while Israel only enrolled 125 000. As for the air force, the Arab countries possessed no less than 937 devices, while Israel had only 326.

Although the Arab numbers seem impressive against the Jewish state, only Egypt had an army worthy of the name in terms of resources and internal organization. It thus sent 140 000 men to fight, Jordan sent 40 000 and Syria sent 32 000, to which would be added 3 000 Iraqi soldiers. But, the Egyptian army suffered from structural problems that caused prejudice, especially due to the fact that it was composed largely of farmers. Moreover, the military hierarchy was respected to the utmost: the officer caste was therefore cut off from the rest of the troop. In addition, the soldiers lacked motivation and training, which was why so many motorized vehicles, such as aircrafts, could not be used. The Syrian and Jordanian ground forces were, in turn, much less numerous and powerful.

The military strategy adopted by the Egyptian and Syrian armies was the same as that of the Soviets at the time, their main features being:

- the success of the counter-attack depended on a large

body of troops;
- powerful artillery;
- ubiquitous armored vehicles;
- the infantry, which was essential, was motorized;
- the artillery and antitank and antiaircraft means were widely used, while aviation was secondary.

As for the Israeli army (IDF), it focused more on the quality of its forces. It was thus composed of a core of professional soldiers that was reinforced by a large number of reservists, called upon when the need arose. The supervision of the IDF soldiers was the key to this system. Officers were constantly placed on the front lines of the battlefield, making them very similar to the ordinary soldiers they were in charge of coaching and encouraging. As for the deployed military strategy, it was essentially dictated by the geographic realities of the territory: in some places, the minimum width actually reached 17 km. All major urban areas were at risk of being too close to the battlefield in the case of invasion. This small size of the territory coupled with a much smaller population than its Arab neighbors imposed four main principles in military matters:

- Combat must preferably take place outside the borders;
- A preventive attack was preferable to a counter-attack;
- The offensive must be swift and decisive, as sustained mobilization could paralyze the country's economy;
- Given its small population, Israel could not go to war against a great power.

It was from these four principles that the Israeli army, mainly through its Chief of Staff Yitzhak Rabin, decided to opt for a strategy based on an air-land battle. Indeed, the Israeli air force had to surpass its competitors' in order to be able to support the advance of ground troops. Once the enemy air forces were destroyed, armored formations were in charge of opening a breach in the enemy camp in order to let the motorized infantry pass, which would then clean the trenches and destroy the enemy artillery. Only after these passages could the infantry completely clear out the enemy positions and occupy the conquered territories.

CHRONOLOGY OF EVENTS: THREE FRONTS INSTEAD OF ONE

Following the pressure from the Israeli public in a tense atmosphere, favored by many provocations from neighboring Arab countries, the Israeli unity government warned IDF troops on Sunday 4th June 1967 that the general offensive would begin the following morning.

On Monday 5 June, the Israeli air force arrived and destroyed the entire Egyptian air force that had remained on the ground in less than three hours. The IDF then sent half of its armored divisions across the Sinai to reach the west bank of the Suez Canal as quickly as possible. The purpose of the war was now to clear the way for the Israeli government: the aim was to provide free access once again to the Red Sea, which had been blocked since 22 May by the Egyptian army that prevented passage to the Tiran Strait. The Israeli government of national unity, led by Levi Eshkol, then explicitly asked King Hussein of Jordan not to intervene in the conflict and assured him that the borders defined by the 1948 war would not be crossed. However, the Jordanian monarch, being allied with Egypt, could not respond favorably to this request. The Jewish neighborhoods of Jerusalem were then bombarded and aerial fights broke out between the Syrians and the Israelis. Israel was no longer committed on a single front, but on two. Although the preemptive strike against Egypt was carefully prepared by the Israeli army, there was nothing prepared for this looming attack on the Israeli-West Bank border. For fear of committing an unprecedented international mistake by sending Israeli troops to attack Jerusalem, Prime Minister Levi Eshkol preferred to wait to consult Defense Minister Moshe Dayan and Chief of Staff Yitzhak Rabin.

On Tuesday 6 June, the Israeli army continued to advance inside the Sinai land on the Egyptian front and the West Bank on the Jordanian front. The enclave of the Gaza Strip was now occupied by the IDF. As for East Jerusalem, Moshe Dayan permitted, without informing the government, paratroopers to circle the walls of the Holy City, but not enter it.

The next day, a great battle involving many armored troops took place in the heart of Sinai. Meanwhile, the Israeli navy took control of the Egyptian city of Sharm-el-Sheikh and, shortly after, the Straits of Tiran were again open to navigation. On the second front, the Israeli counter-attack was incredibly effective: in the late afternoon, the IDF held all major cities of the West Bank and could reach the Jordan (Middle Eastern river). Jerusalem was also entirely in the hands of the Israelis 10 hours after Moshe Dayan gave the order to take the city, again without warning the Israeli government. Three hours later, Moshe Dayan, Yitzhak Rabin, Levi Eshkol and the rest of the government travelled to the Wailing Wall to pray. Prime Minister Levi Eshkol said at the time that "Israel did not expect territorial gains from this war", to which Moshe Dayan publicly replied: "We have returned to all that is holy in our land. We have returned never to be parted from it again" (Gurgand, 1967). Israel then obtained a cease-fire from Jordan.

On Thursday 8 June, the Israelis reached the Suez Canal: the Sinai battle was over and Gamal Abdel Nasser in turn accepted the truce.

Once the Jordanian and Egyptian armies had retreated, Israel had yet to address the issue of Syria. Although the Syrians were instrumental in installing the tense climate that preceded the Six-Day War, they were not yet actually involved in the conflict. The government of Levi Eshkol was thus opposed to the idea of attacking Syria, especially since the country's links with the Soviet Union were so strong. In any case, it eventually yielded to the pressure of the population residing near the Syrian border, but also of the military leaders, including Moshe Dayan. The IDF entered Golan Heights on Friday 9 June.

Good to know

Golan Heights, located at the crossroads of Syria, Lebanon, Jordan and Israel, was undoubtedly an important strategic location for the region. Located in the northern part of the Jordan River, between the slopes of Mount Hermon and the Yarmouk River, the Golan Heights extended to the eastern shores of Lake Tiberias. Having control of this territory would therefore provide them with the benefit of a height advantage over the rest of the neighboring countries and the ability to prevent any land attack. Also, thanks to the Jordan River and some of its tributaries, the rich soil made for good farming and ranching, which was not insignificant.

On Saturday 10 June, the Syrians surrendered facing the IDF attack in the Golan Heights, which then became a part of Israel. This latest Israeli victory thus marked the end of the Six-Day War.

THE OUTCOME OF THE BATTLE

The Israeli victory came at a price, since the IDF recorded no less than 679 deaths on the battlefield and another 150 wounded. However, the Arab belligerents suffered the most significant losses:

- Egypt did not record its casualties, however it is estimated that between 5 000 and 10 000 soldiers lost their lives;
- Jordan lost 700 soldiers and 550 were taken prisoner;
- Syria counted 450 dead and 570 taken prisoner.

The record of the Israeli territorial conquests is significant as a result of the lightning war that lasted only 132 hours: the area of land controlled by Israel had quadrupled from 20 700 km² to 88 500 km². This increase made the defense of the territory of the Jewish state easier: the Suez Canal and the Sinai desert on the one side, and the Golan Heights on the other formed natural borders that made any invasions more difficult. Also, the new terms of the cease-fire prevented any possibility of a surprise attack by Egypt, Syria or Jordan.

REPERCUSSIONS OF THE WAR

OPENNESS TO RELIGIOUS RADICALISM IN THE ARAB WORLD

For the belligerent Arab countries, the situation just after the Six-Day War was critical, as the Arab military weakness had been exposed. These people who had believed that they were militarily powerful, as stated by their respective governments, took this failure as a sign of deception and revolted. A Kuwaiti journalist said: "We have been led to believe [by Arab propaganda] that we could liquidate Israel in just three hours, when within three hours, Israel has suddenly humiliated us" (Hazan 2001, p. 64).

This failure marked the end of the Pan-Arab secular nationalism of which Nasser was the figurehead and opened the way for the fundamentalist Islamic movement represented by the Muslim Brotherhood. The Islamists, full of nostalgia, refused this defeat and denied the facts. Gradually, their movement gained power and they attempted to erase the visible traces of the West in everyday life. The Six-Day War thus announced the rejection of the West and of secularism in the Arab world.

A WAR THAT LED TO MANY OTHERS

Although this victory had a euphoric effect for the Israelis who hoped that the neighboring Arab countries would finally recognize the existence of their state, the Khartoum summit, which brought together all the Arab leaders from

29 August to 1 September 1967, proved otherwise. A triple "no" closed the assembly, which was humiliated by this second heavy military defeat against the Jewish state: no to peace with Israel, no to the recognition of Israel as a state, and no to any negotiations with Israel. The entire Arab world fully intended to recover the newly occupied territories from the Israelis.

Good to know

The Khartoum summit aimed to define the economic and military policies that each of the eight Arab country participants must follow in order to carry out the struggle against Israel. The recovery of lost territory was also an important point. During this meeting, all political differences were forgotten and true Arab solidarity appeared. Thus, from an economic point of view, Saudi Arabia, Libya and Kuwait all agreed to donate 20% of their oil revenues to countries that had suffered from the war, in order to rebuild their armies as quickly as possible. A military agreement was also established with the promise of collaboration in the event of a new conflict with Israel.

Faced with such a categorical response, Israel hid behind an equally determined attitude by deciding to colonize and integrate the new conquered territories as quickly as possible, which further complicated diplomatic conflict resolution. It was therefore not until a few months later, on 22 November 1967, that a compromise text drafted by the United Nations

Security Council was proposed to both parties. The text, called Resolution 242, was extremely vague, allowing each of the opponents to find it suitable.

In addition to a reminder of the freedom of navigation through international waterways, meaning the Suez Canal and the Straits of Tiran, and a call for the recognition of all states of the region and their territorial integrity, Resolution 242 evoked the need for a withdrawal of the Israeli army from the newly conquered territories, as well as the establi-shment of secure and recognized borders by other nations. However, nowhere in the text were these famous occupied territories or boundaries clearly defined. Israel saw this as an authorization of direct negotiations with the Arab countries and refused to retreat behind the pre-war borders. For their part, the Arab states were strongly opposed to any talks until the IDF had left the territories of the Sinai, the Golan Heights, the Gaza Strip and the West Bank.

Gamal Abdel Nasser then engaged in a war of attrition with Israel at the beginning of the following year along the Suez Canal, where clashes were multiplying. This qualification of the war was also used by the Egyptian President himself, who said in 1969: "I cannot invade the Sinai, but I can break down the morale of Israel through attrition" (Josette, 1969). Conflict persisted until the end of July 1970, when a cease-fire was established, once again for the benefit of the Jewish state.

Three years later, on 6 October 1973, the Egyptians and the Syrians began a new war, on the same day as the fast of *Yom Kippur* ('Atonement') simultaneously directing a surprise attack on the Sinai Peninsula and the Golan Heights. The fighting lasted for just under three weeks and Israel emerged victorious once again. However, their victory was more difficult to claim than it had been in previous conflicts. Part of the Israeli government, including Moshe Dayan – who was still Defense Minister – was forced to resign following this blatant lack of anticipation in military matters.

Finally, in 1978 the Egyptian-Israeli conflict was buried with the Camp David Accords: the Sinai land was returned to Egypt, which finally recognized the existence of the state of Israel.

THE PALESTINIANS: FORGOTTEN AFTER THE CONFLICT

After the Six-Day War, the fate of the Palestinians was only briefly mentioned, both in the Middle East and on the international scene. Thus, even in Resolution 242 of the UN, they only appeared when it came to finding a solution regarding the exodus of more than a million Palestinians who left the territories newly occupied by the Israeli army. However, the text called for the establishment of demilitarized zones and a settlement of the refugee issue. It should be noted that neither Palestine nor Syria agreed to sign Resolution 242.

Besides, although this crushing defeat came as a trauma for the entire Arab population, the Palestinians were also in shock. The Six-Day War and the war of attrition that followed had the effect of reinforcing a new generation of Palestinian militants who now did not believe in the liberation of Palestine through any Arab unity anymore. Therefore, the different Palestinian movements were reorganized in 1968 into a new Palestine Liberation Organization (PLO), joined by *Fatah* (Movement of the National Liberation of Palestine), including Yasser Arafat (1929-2004) who became president.

The PLO decided to adopt a strategy independent of other Arab states, using terrorism on a global scale in order to obtain the recognition of the Palestinian state and the territory it controlled. However, this approach undermined the different neighboring states that hosted Palestinian refugees, as they gave the impression of acting as an independent state within another state. Although Lebanon was too weak to react, Jordan was not: in September 1970, the Jordanian army began the dissolution of the Palestinian infrastructure on its territory in a pure bloodbath. The PLO, decimated, then found refuge in Lebanon, but nonetheless continued its actions for a free Palestine.

The Six-Day War and the colonization of territories populated mainly by Palestinians therefore had the effect of definitively asserting the existence of an Arab national identity in Palestine, while catalyzing this around the Palestinian nationalism of the PLO and the outstanding figure of Yasser Arafat, instead of around the idea of a united Arab League.

SUMMARY

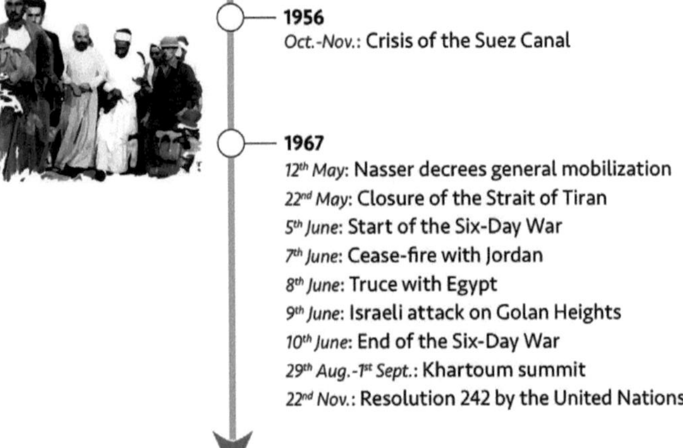

1956
Oct.-Nov.: Crisis of the Suez Canal

1967
12th May: Nasser decrees general mobilization
22nd May: Closure of the Strait of Tiran
5th June: Start of the Six-Day War
7th June: Cease-fire with Jordan
8th June: Truce with Egypt
9th June: Israeli attack on Golan Heights
10th June: End of the Six-Day War
29th Aug.-1st Sept.: Khartoum summit
22nd Nov.: Resolution 242 by the United Nations

- Following the wave of anti-Semitic violence raging in Europe, a Zionist movement gradually began the restoration of a Jewish state in Palestine in the late 19th century.
- Jewish immigration to Palestine increased particularly with the rise to power of Adolf Hitler and Nazism: tensions therefore grew.
- Three major crises then occurred: the Arab revolt in Palestine (1936-1938), the War of Independence in 1948, following which Israel occupied 78% of Palestine, and the crisis of the Suez Canal (1956), which opposed Egypt to Israel, Britain and France.
- To this tense context, tensions along the Israeli-Syrian border and the fear of the Egyptians of the development

of Israel's nuclear weapons were added.

- On 22 May 1967, the Egyptian President declared the closure of the Strait of Tiran, which prevented the Israelis from accessing the Red Sea. Therefore, disguised threats were exchanged on both sides and the Israeli public urged the government to act. On 4 June 1967, the IDF was ordered to begin the offensive against Egypt the following day.
- On 5 June 1967, the IDF destroyed the Egyptian air force in only three hours, before sending half of its armed forces throughout the Sinai in order to ensure free access to the Strait of Tiran again. Immediately, Jordan and Syria declared war on Israel and Jordan engaged in combat.
- The advance of the Israeli troops in the Sinai and the West Bank territories continued and, on 7 June, Jerusalem and the entire West Bank territory, to Jordan, fell into the hands of the IDF: Israel thus obtained a cease-fire from Jordan.
- The next day, the Israeli army reached the Suez Canal and a truce was accepted by the Egyptians.
- The only problem that remained to be solved was that of Syria, as the country had not initiated any combat. However, popular pressure was so high that the Israeli government decided, on 9 June, to begin an offensive in the Golan Heights. But the attack ended in failure, marking the end of the Six-Day War.
- Israel saw its territory quadruple in size and the failure of the belligerent Arab countries signaled the end of the Pan-Arab secular nationalism, leaving the way open to the fundamentalist Islamist movement of the Muslim Brotherhood.

- In order to calm the situation, the United Nations prepared a peace text, Resolution 242, but the content was so vague that tensions continued to grow, and it was not until 1978 that the Israeli-Egyptian conflict was finally buried with the Camp David Accords.
- Largely forgotten, the Palestinians were only briefly mentioned, both in the Middle East and on the international scene. Disappointed, they then decided to come together in 1968 in a new Palestine Liberation Organization, whose strategy was now independent of other Arab States.

FIND OUT MORE

BIBLIOGRAPHY

- Abitbol, M. (2007) *Juifs et Arabes au XXe siècle*. Paris: Perrin.
- Bamavi, Elie (2007) 5 juin 1967 : Israël attaque. *L'Histoire*. Volume 321, pp. 32-33.
- Burrowes, R. and Douglas, M. (1972) 'The Road to the Six Day War: Towards an Enumerative History of Four Arab States and Israel, 1965-1967'. *The Journal of Conflict Resolution*. 16(2), pp. 211-226.
- Charfi, M. (2007) Du côté des Arabes : l'insupportable défaite. *L'Histoire*. Volume 321, pp. 50-52.
- Defay, A. (2011) *Géopolitique du Proche-Orient*. Paris: Presses Universitaires de France.
- Duclos, L.-J. (1979) La "guerre d'usure" égypto-israélienne, 1968-1970. *Études internationales*. 10(1), pp. 127-175.
- Gurgand, J.-N. (1967) Cette victoire, nous la devons à nous seuls. *L'Express*. [Online]. [Accessed 6 December 2016]. Available from: <http://www.lexpress.fr/actualite/monde/proche-moyen-orient/cette-victoire-nous-la-devons-a-nous-seuls_490433.html>
- Josette, A. (1969) La nouvelle armée de Nasser. *Le Nouvel Observateur*. 11 August.
- Kurtulus, E.N. (2007) The Notion of a "Pre-Emptive War": the Six-Day War Revisited. *Middle East Journal*. 61(2), pp. 220-238.
- Le Gac, D. and Kauffmann, J.-P. (1975) *Juifs et Arabes en Palestine*. Paris: Le Centurion.

- Picard, E. (2006) *La politique dans le monde arabe*. Paris: Armand Colin.
- Popp, R. (2006) Stumbling Decidedly into the Six-Day War. *The Middle East Journal*. 60(2), pp. 281-309.
- Razoux, P. (2004) *La guerre des Six Jours (5-10 juin 1967). Du mythe à la réalité*. Paris: Economica.
- Peretz, P. (2007) Six jours qui ont remodelé la carte du Proche-Orient. *L'Histoire*. Volume 321, pp. 34-41.
- Saadoun, H. (2003) L'hostilité croissante. L'élément palestinien et la fin des communautés juives en terre d'Islam (1920-1967). *Pardès*. Volume 34, pp. 25-32.
- Shimoni, Y. (1991) *Biographical Dictionary of the Middle East*. New York: Facts on File.
- Stein, L. (2009) *The Making of Modern Israel: 1948-1967*. Cambridge: Polity Press.

ADDITIONAL SOURCES

- Bowen, J. (2004) *Six Days: How the 1967 War Shaped the Middle East*. London: Simon and Schuster.
- Gresh, A. and Vidal, D. (2004) *The New A-Z of the Middle East*. London: I.B. Tauris & Co Ltd.
- Oran, M.B. (2002) *Six Days of War: June 1967 and the Making of the Modern Middle East*. Oxford: Oxford University Press.
- Segev, T. (2008) *1967: Israel, the War and the Year that Transformed the Middle East*. London: Abacus.

ICONOGRAPHIC SOURCES

- Arab revolt against British occupation. Royalty-free

reproduction picture.
- Portrait of Gamal Abdel Nasser. Royalty-free reproduction picture.
- Portrait of Levi Eshkol. Royalty-free reproduction picture.
- Portrait of Moshe Dayan. Royalty-free reproduction picture.

DOCUMENTARIES AND PHOTO REPORTS

- Collection of photographs by Gilles Caron, photojournalist who covered the Six-Day War by following the Israeli army.
- *La Guerre des Six Jours.* (1967) [Television program]. France: Actualités françaises.
- *Six Days to Eternity.* (1969) [Documentary]. Yakov Hameiri and Tova Biran. Dir. Israel: Brummer Film Productions Ltd.
- *Six Days in June.* (2007) [Documentary]. Ilan Ziv. Dir. Canada/France/Israel: Alma Films, Instinct Films, Point du Jour.

MUSEUMS, MONUMENTS AND COMMEMORATIVE EVENTS

- Ammunition Hill Memorial and Museum in Jerusalem, former stronghold of the Jordanian army base turned into a museum and memorial site of the Israeli capture of Jerusalem during the Six-Day War (Palestine).
- The memorial of the 84th Division, which contributed to the Israeli victory over the Egyptian army in the land of

Sinai, in the region of the Negev (Southern Israel).

- The Army Museum in Damascus, which includes a room devoted to the weapons used during the Six-Day War (Syria).
- *Naksa Day* (which means "day of failure") is celebrated every 5th June by the Palestinians.

IMPROVE YOUR GENERAL KNOWLEDGE

IN A BLINK OF AN EYE !

www.50minutes.com